SIMPLE MACHINES

levers

VALERIE BODDEN

Published by Creative Education
P.O. Box 227, Mankato, Minnesota 56002
Creative Education is an imprint of The Creative Company
www.thecreativecompany.us

Design and production by Liddy Walseth
Art direction by Rita Marshall
Printed by Corporate Graphics in the United States of America

Photographs by Dreamstime (Viktor Gmyria, Mark Stout), Getty Images
(Altrendo Images, French School, Patti McConville, Ryan McVay, Rod Morata,
Matthew Paul, Petrified Collection, Jeff Smith, Diego Uchitel), iStockphoto
(Steve Cukrov, Diane Diederich, Donald Erickson, Rich Koele, Marco
Maccarini), James P. Rowan Photography

Library of Congress Cataloging-in-Publication Data
Bodden, Valerie.
Levers / by Valerie Bodden.
p. cm. — (Simple machines)
Summary: A foundational look at levers, explaining how these simple machines
work and describing some common examples, such as crowbars, that have been
used throughout history.
Includes index.
ISBN 978-1-60818-009-7
1. Levers—Juvenile literature. I. Title. II. Series.
TJ147.B62 2011
621.8—dc22   2009048838
CPSIA: 040110 PO1140

First Edition
2 4 6 8 9 7 5 3 1

CREATIVE ☙ EDUCATION

SIMPLE MACHINES

levers

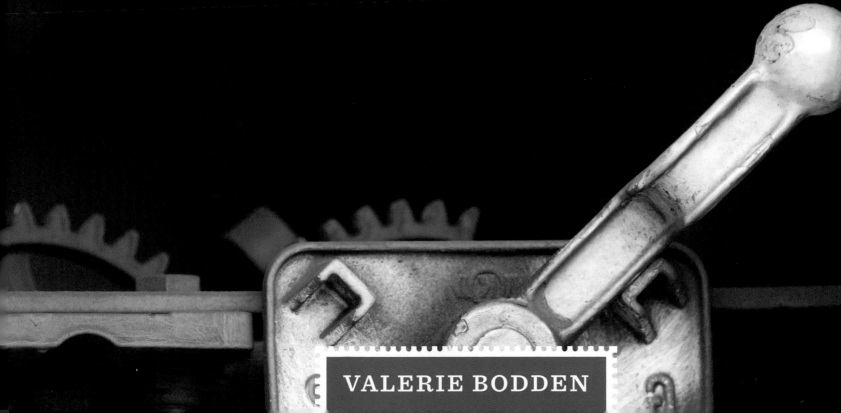

VALERIE BODDEN

contents

Have you ever played on a seesaw or rowed a boat? You might not have known it, but you were using a lever. A lever makes lifting or moving objects easier.

A lever is a kind of simple machine. Simple machines have only a few moving parts. Some have no moving parts at all. Simple machines help people do WORK.

Some levers look like handles on machines

A lever is made up of a bar that rests on a **FULCRUM** (*FUL-krum*). On a seesaw, the fulcrum is the stand that holds the seesaw up. A fulcrum can be in the middle of the lever. Or it can be closer to one end.

A crane
is a lever
that lifts
heavy
objects

10

Levers can be used to lift objects. One end of the lever is placed under the object. Then a person pushes down on the other end of the lever. As that end of the lever goes down, the lever turns on the fulcrum. The end with the object moves up.

If the fulcrum of a lever is placed close to an object, the object will be easier to lift. If the fulcrum is farther away from the object, you will have to push harder on the lever. But you will not have to push down as far.

Levers come in all colors and sizes

Oars row boats, while some crow-bars take out nails

People have been using levers for thousands of years. **CROWBARS** were some of the first levers. The **OARS** of boats were also early levers.

Today, people still use levers. The back of a hammer is a lever that lifts nails out of wood. A wheelbarrow is a lever, too. The wheel acts as the fulcrum.

A door is also a lever. The **HINGE** is the fulcrum. Even your arm is a lever—with your elbow as the fulcrum.

A door hinge and an elbow work the same way

Some tools are made of two levers put together. A scissors is made of two levers. So is a nutcracker. Levers are everywhere. Without them, we would have a much harder time moving the objects around us!

A CLOSER LOOK at *Levers*

TO LEARN MORE ABOUT HOW THE **POSITION** OF THE FULCRUM AFFECTS A LEVER, TRY TO CUT THROUGH 10 SHEETS OF PAPER. FIRST, OPEN YOUR SCISSORS WIDE AND PLACE THE PAPER CLOSE TO THE FULCRUM (WHERE THE BLADES CROSS). TRY TO CUT THE PAPER. THEN PLACE THE PAPER CLOSE TO THE BLADE TIPS AND CUT AGAIN. IS THE PAPER EASIER TO CUT WHEN IT IS CLOSER TO THE FULCRUM OR FAR FROM IT?

Glossary

crowbars—long bars that are placed under objects to help lift them
fulcrum—the point a lever rests on and turns around
hinge—the metal parts that hold a door to its frame and allow it to swing open and shut
oars—long poles that are flat on one end and are pushed through water to move a boat forward
position—the spot where something is placed
work—using force (a push or pull) to move an object

Read More

Oxlade, Chris. *Levers*. Chicago: Heinemann Library, 2003.
Thales, Sharon. *Levers to the Rescue*. Mankato, Minn.: Capstone Press, 2007.

Web Sites

MIKIDS.com
http://www.mikids.com/Smachines.htm
Learn about the six kinds of simple machines and see examples of each one.

Simple Machines
http://staff.harrisonburg.k12.va.us/~mwampole/1-resources/simple-machines/index.html
Try to figure out which common objects are simple machines.

Index